NFL TEAMS

BY ALLAN MOREY

THE BALTIMORE RAVENS STORY

TORQUE™

BELLWETHER MEDIA · MINNEAPOLIS, MN

Are you ready to take it to the extreme? Torque books thrust you into the action-packed world of sports, vehicles, mystery, and adventure. These books may include dirt, smoke, fire, and chilling tales. **WARNING**: read at your own risk.

This edition first published in 2017 by Bellwether Media, Inc.

Library of Congress Cataloging-in-Publication Data

Names: Morey, Allan, author.
Title: The Baltimore Ravens Story / by Allan Morey.
Description: Minneapolis, MN : Bellwether Media, Inc., 2017. | Series: Torque: NFL Teams | Includes index.
Identifiers: LCCN 2015041465 | ISBN 9781626173576 (hardcover : alk. paper)
Subjects: LCSH: Baltimore Ravens (Football team)–History–Juvenile literature.
Classification: LCC GV956.B3 M67 2017 | DDC 796.332/64097526–dc23
LC record available at http://lccn.loc.gov/2015041465

Printed in the United States of America, North Mankato, MN.

TABLE OF CONTENTS

It is **Super Bowl** 47. The Baltimore Ravens face the San Francisco 49ers. The Ravens score first. **Quarterback** Joe Flacco tosses a 13-yard pass to **wide receiver** Anquan Boldin. Touchdown!

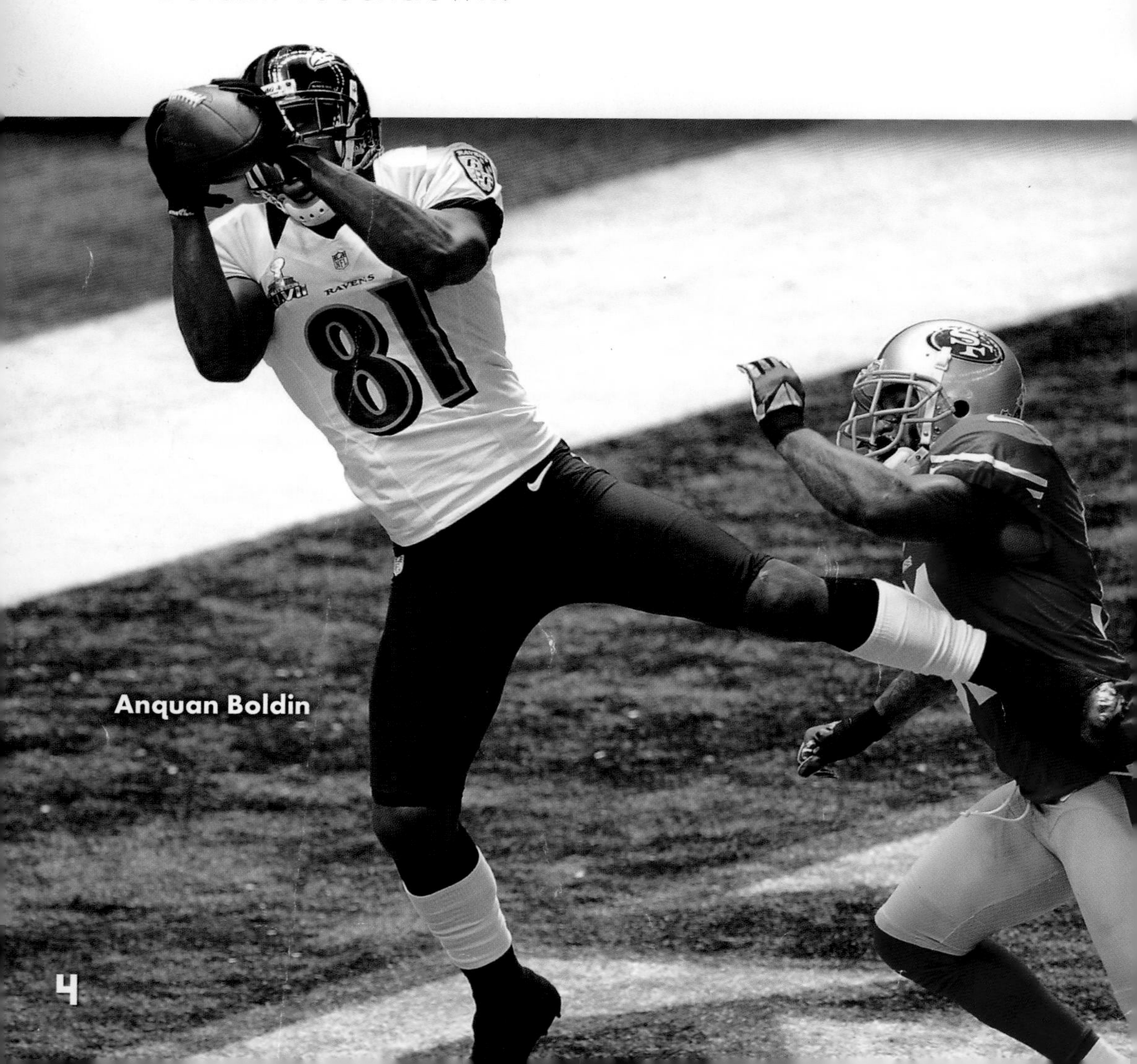

Anquan Boldin

Joe Flacco

In the first half, the 49ers kick two field goals. Flacco throws two more touchdowns. The score is 21 to 6.

SUPER BOWL RECORD

The kickoff return by Jones was 108 yards. That is a Super Bowl record!

Wide receiver Jacoby Jones starts the second half with a big play for the Ravens. He returns a kickoff for a touchdown!

Then the 49ers finally start scoring. With minutes left in the game, they are down by only 5 points. But the Ravens' **defense** clamps down. The Ravens become Super Bowl champions!

SCORING TERMS

END ZONE

the area at each end of a football field; a team scores by entering the opponent's end zone with the football.

EXTRA POINT

a score that occurs when a kicker kicks the ball between the opponent's goal posts after a touchdown is scored; 1 point.

FIELD GOAL

a score that occurs when a kicker kicks the ball between the opponent's goal posts; 3 points.

SAFETY

a score that occurs when a player on offense is tackled behind his own goal line; 2 points for defense.

TOUCHDOWN

a score that occurs when a team crosses into its opponent's end zone with the football; 6 points.

TWO-POINT CONVERSION

a score that occurs when a team crosses into its opponent's end zone with the football after scoring a touchdown; 2 points.

DOMINATING DEFENSE

SUPER BOWL 47
FEBRUARY 3, 2013

Defense has been the name of the game for the Ravens. From Ed Reed to C.J. Mosley, the team has always been loaded with defensive stars.

The Ravens used their crushing "D" to win two Super Bowls. They won in 2001. Then they did it again in 2013.

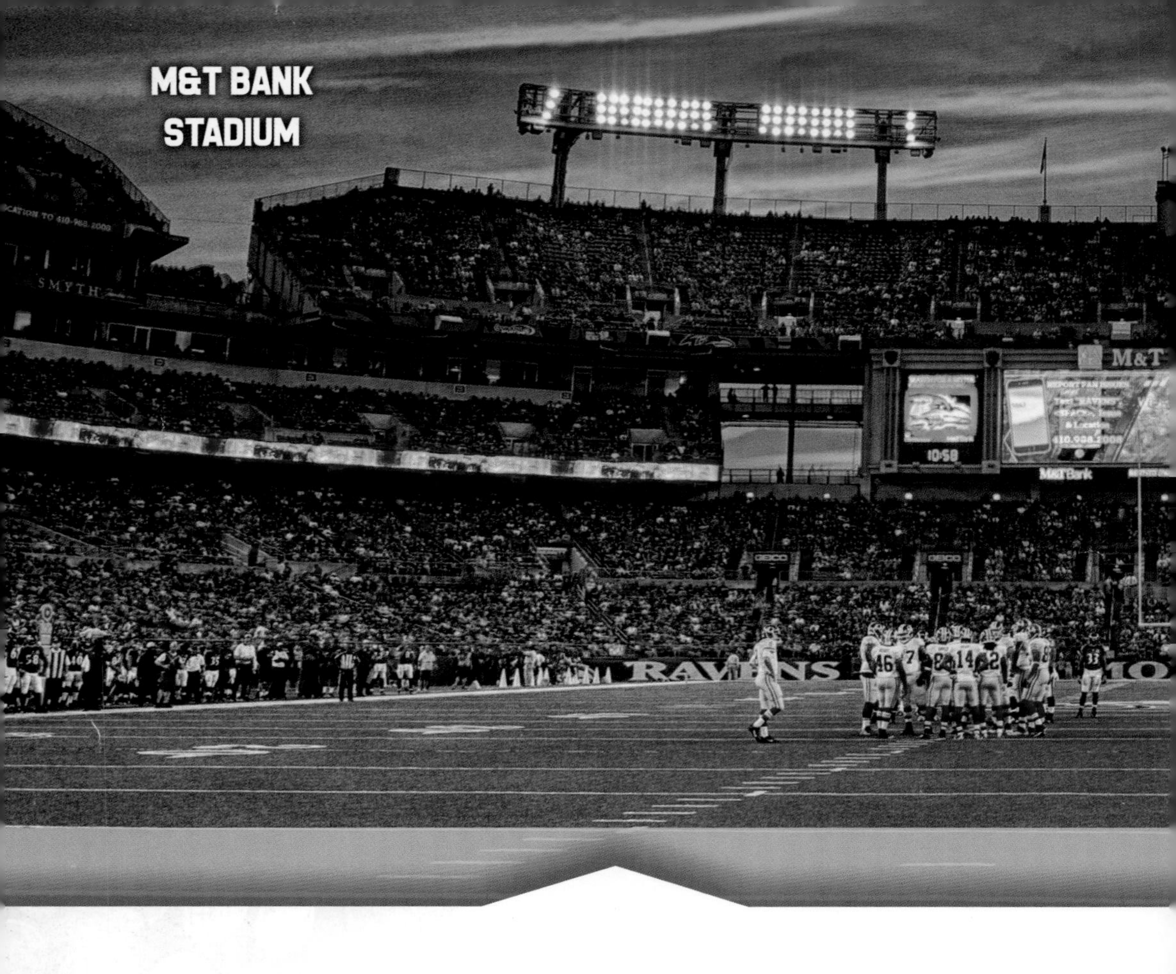

M&T BANK STADIUM

Baltimore, Maryland, is a seaport city with a lot of history. Its connection with the National Football League (NFL) started with the Colts in the early 1950s. That team called the city home until moving to Indianapolis, Indiana, in 1984.

The Ravens became Baltimore's team in the late 1990s. They play at Baltimore's M&T Bank Stadium.

THE RAVENS

The Ravens take their name from Edgar Allan Poe's famous poem called "The Raven." Poe spent many years of his early life in Baltimore.

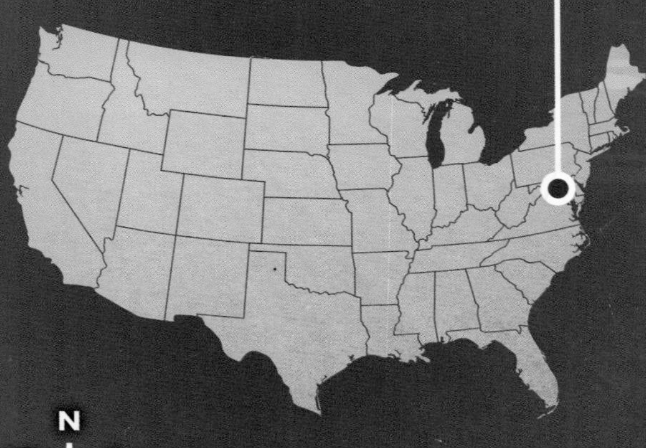

The Ravens joined the NFL in 1996. They play in the American Football **Conference** (AFC). They are part of the North **Division**.

The division includes the Pittsburgh Steelers, Cleveland Browns, and Cincinnati Bengals. Many fans see the Steelers and Browns as the Ravens' biggest **rivals**.

FIRST LOSS

The Ravens' first-ever loss came at the hands of the Steelers.

NFC

NFC NORTH

CHICAGO **BEARS**

DETROIT **LIONS**

GREEN BAY **PACKERS**

MINNESOTA **VIKINGS**

NFC EAST

DALLAS **COWBOYS**

NEW YORK **GIANTS**

PHILADELPHIA **EAGLES**

WASHINGTON **REDSKINS**

NFC SOUTH

ATLANTA **FALCONS**

CAROLINA **PANTHERS**

NEW ORLEANS **SAINTS**

TAMPA BAY **BUCCANEERS**

NFC WEST

ARIZONA **CARDINALS**

LOS ANGELES **RAMS**

SAN FRANCISCO **49ERS**

SEATTLE **SEAHAWKS**

In 1996, Cleveland Browns owner Art Modell moved his players and coaches to Baltimore. This was the start of the Baltimore Ravens.

The Ravens struggled at first. But they quickly built one of the league's best defenses. Some call their defense from the 2000 season one of the best of all time.

Art Modell

Riddell
22
55
RAVENS
THRA

In 2008, the Ravens hired head coach John Harbaugh. They also **drafted** quarterback Joe Flacco. This pair helped make the team a success.

John Harbaugh

BATTLE BETWEEN BROTHERS

Super Bowl 47 was called the Harbaugh Bowl. The Ravens and 49ers were coached by brothers John and Jim.

Joe Flacco

The Ravens went to the **playoffs** after the next five seasons. They capped it off by winning Super Bowl 47.

RAVENS

TIMELINE

1996

Joined the NFL

1999

Hired head coach Brian Billick

2001

Won Super Bowl 35, beating the New York Giants

34 FINAL SCORE 7

1998

First played in M&T Bank Stadium

2000

Held opponents to only 165 points all season (NFL record)

2002

Drafted safety Ed Reed

2013

Won Super Bowl 47, beating the San Francisco 49ers

34 FINAL SCORE 31

2008

Hired head coach John Harbaugh

2008

Drafted quarterback Joe Flacco

2008

Celebrated the retirement of Hall-of-Fame offensive lineman Jonathan Ogden

The Ravens have had their share of superstars. **Linebacker** Ray Lewis was a tackling machine on defense during both Super Bowl wins.

Ray Lewis

Ed Reed

Ed Reed joined the Ravens in 2002. He may have been the greatest **safety** of his time. He picked off 61 passes with the Ravens!

Jonathan Ogden anchored the Ravens' **offensive line** for 12 seasons. He was a **Pro Bowler** 11 times and is now a member of the Pro Football Hall of Fame.

Today, quarterback Joe Flacco is one of football's great **clutch** passers. He wins big games for the Ravens. His playoff record is among the best in the NFL.

TEAM GREATS

JONATHAN OGDEN
OFFENSIVE TACKLE
1996-2007

RAY LEWIS
LINEBACKER
1996-2012

JAMAL LEWIS
RUNNING BACK
2000-2006

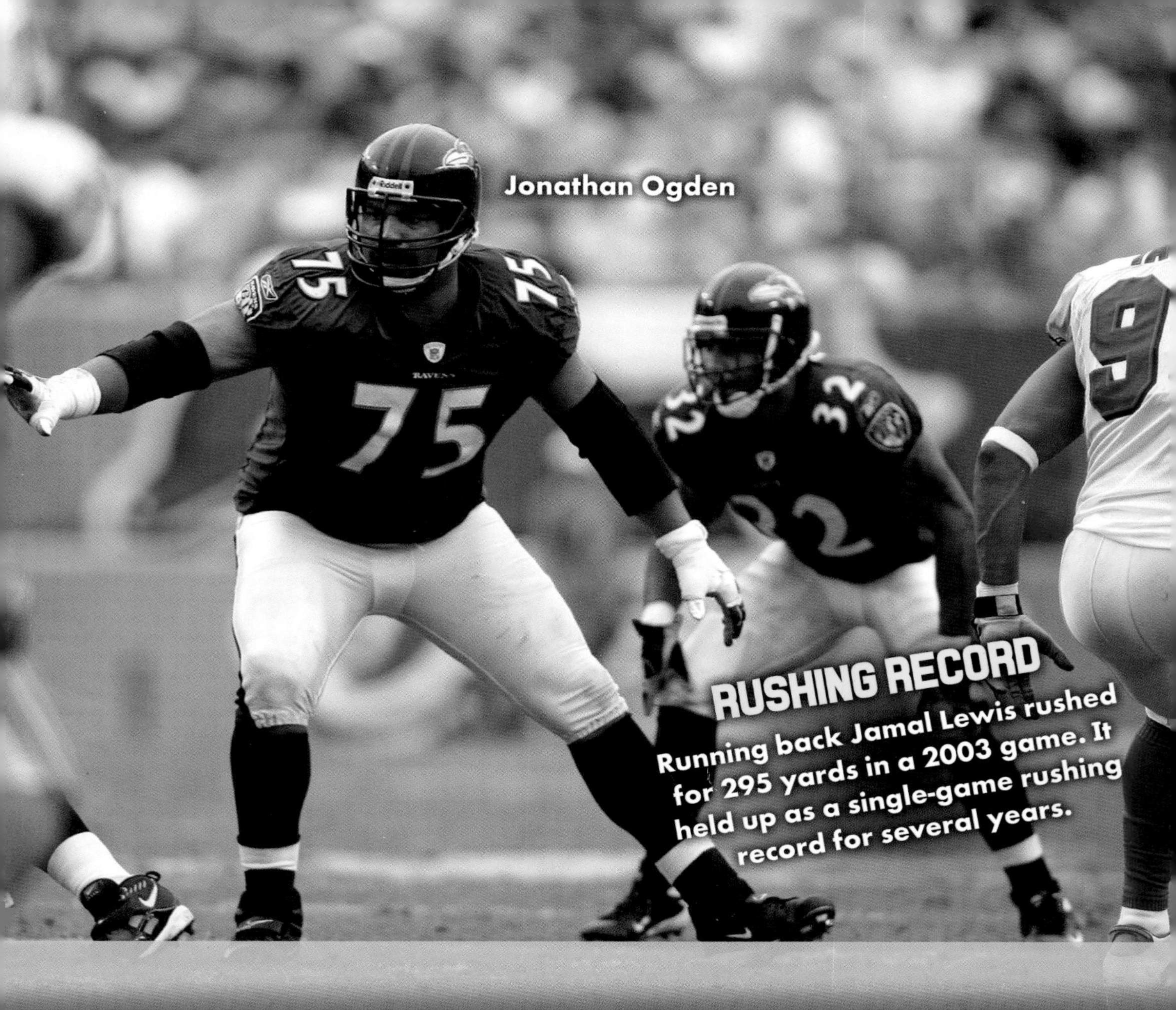
Jonathan Ogden

RUSHING RECORD

Running back Jamal Lewis rushed for 295 yards in a 2003 game. It held up as a single-game rushing record for several years.

20 ED REED
SAFETY
2002-2012

5 JOE FLACCO
QUARTERBACK
2008-PRESENT

57 C.J. MOSLEY
LINEBACKER
2014-PRESENT

For Ravens fans, the fun starts before game day. Many in Baltimore support their team on Purple Friday. They wear purple to work and school.

On game days, Baltimore turns into a top **tailgating** city. Rain, snow, or shine, fans come together. Many fire up their grills to cook crab cakes!

At home games, Baltimore's Marching Ravens help fans get charged up. The team band features more than 150 musicians and crew members.

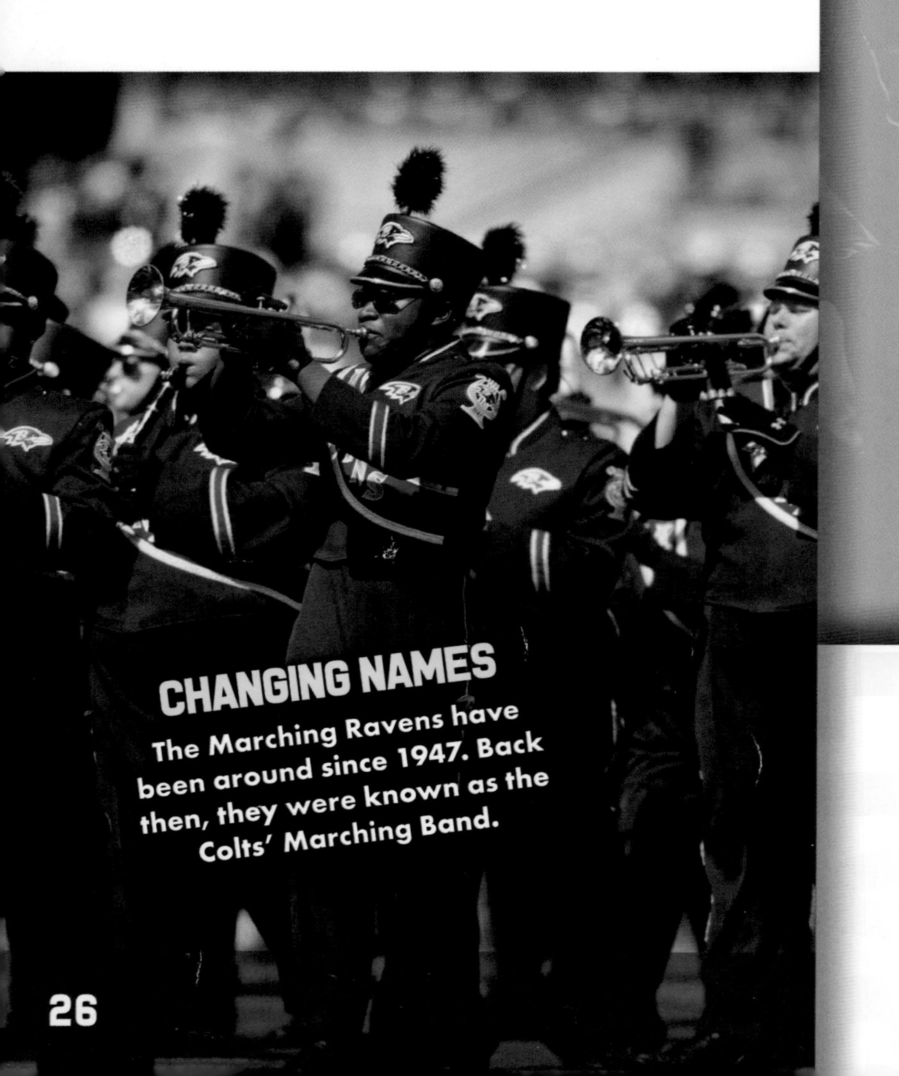

CHANGING NAMES

The Marching Ravens have been around since 1947. Back then, they were known as the Colts' Marching Band.

Fans love to sing along with "The Baltimore Fight Song." They belt out, "Fight! Fight! Fight!" as they cheer their team to victory.

MORE ABOUT THE

RAVENS

Team name:
Baltimore Ravens

Team name explained:
Named for Edgar Allan Poe's poem, "The Raven"

Nickname:
Purple Pain

Joined NFL: **1996**

Conference: **AFC**

Division: **North**

Main rivals: **Pittsburgh Steelers, Cleveland Browns**

Hometown: Baltimore, Maryland

Training camp location: Under Armour Performance Center, Owings Mills, Maryland

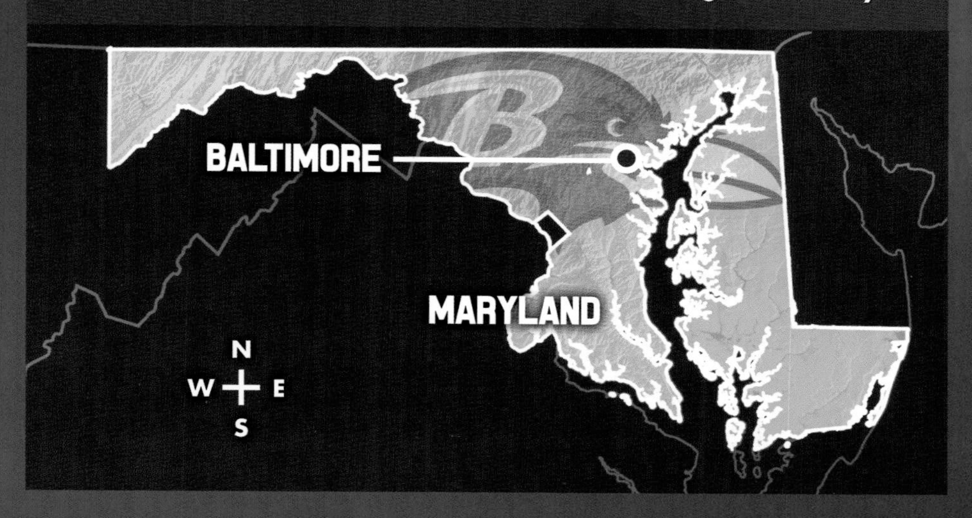

Home stadium name: M&T Bank Stadium

Stadium opened: 1998

Seats in stadium: 71,008

Logo: A purple raven's head with the letter B for Baltimore

Colors: Purple, black, metallic gold

Mascots: Poe and ravens, Rise and Conquer

GLOSSARY

clutch—able to do well during a critical time or situation

conference—a large grouping of sports teams that often play one another

defense—the group of players who try to stop opposing teams from scoring

division—a small grouping of sports teams that often play one another; usually there are several divisions of teams in a conference.

drafted—chose a college athlete to play for a professional team

linebacker—a player on defense whose main job is to make tackles and stop passes; a linebacker stands just behind the defensive linemen.

offensive line—players on offense whose main jobs are to protect the quarterback and to block for running backs

playoffs—the games played after the regular NFL season is over; playoff games determine which teams play in the Super Bowl.

Pro Bowler—a player who makes the Pro Bowl, the NFL's all-star game

quarterback—a player on offense whose main job is to throw and hand off the ball

rivals—teams that are long-standing opponents

safety—a player on defense whose main job is to prevent wide receivers from catching the ball; a safety is positioned behind all the other players on defense.

Super Bowl—the championship game for the NFL

tailgating—enjoying pregame time by having a cookout in a parking lot at a sporting event; a tailgate is also the door at the back of a pickup truck that flips down.

wide receiver—a player on offense whose main job is to catch passes from the quarterback

TO LEARN MORE

AT THE LIBRARY

Aretha, David. *Joe Flacco.* New York, N.Y.: Bearport Publishing, 2015.

Burgess, Zack. *Meet the Baltimore Ravens.* Chicago, Ill.: Norwood House Press, 2016.

Nagelhout, Ryan. *Joe Flacco.* New York, N.Y.: Gareth Stevens Publishing, 2014.

ON THE WEB

Learning more about the Baltimore Ravens is as easy as 1, 2, 3.

1. Go to www.factsurfer.com.

2. Enter "Baltimore Ravens" into the search box.

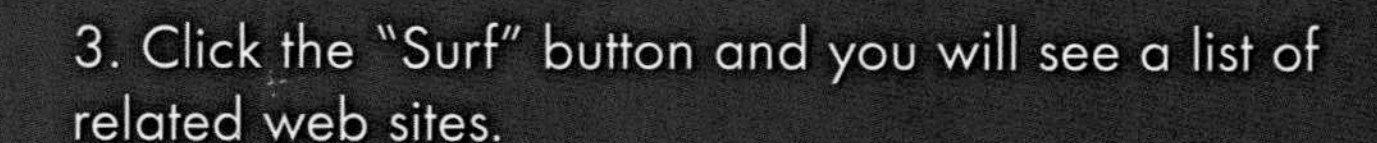
3. Click the "Surf" button and you will see a list of related web sites.

With factsurfer.com, finding more information is just a click away.

INDEX

The images in this book are reproduced through the courtesy of: Corbis, front cover, pp. 6-7, 10-11, 18 (top), 22 (middle), 24, 26-27; Tribune Content Agency LLC/ Alamy, pp. 4-5, 12-13, 16, 18 (bottom right); Tannen Maury/ EPA/ Newscom, p. 5; Perry Knotts/ AP Images, p. 7; Erik S. Lesser/ EPA/ Newscom, pp. 8-9; Deposit Photos/ Glow Images, pp. 12-13 (logos), 18-19 (logos), 28-29 (logos); George Bridges/ KRT/ Newscom, p. 14; Rob Tringall, Jr./ SportsChrome/ Newscom, p. 15; Chris Granger/ Polaris/ Newscom, pp. 16-17; Rich Kane/ AI Wire Photo Service/ Newscom, p. 18 (bottom left); John Cetrino/ EPA/ Newscom, p. 19 (top left); Larry W. Smith/ EPA/ Newscom, p. 19 (top right); Scott A. Miller/ ZUMA Press/ Alamy, p. 19 (bottom left); J.C. Ridley/ Cal Sport Media/ Newscom, pp. 19 (bottom right), 22-23; Jeff Lewis/ Icon SMI/ Photoshot/ Newscom, p. 20-21; The Palm Beach Post/ ZUMA Press/ Alamy, p. 21; Edward Larson/ AI Wire Photo Service/ Newscom, p. 22 (left); Ed Wolfstein/ EPA/ Newscom, p. 22 (right); TJ Root/ Southcreek/ ZUMA Press/ Alamy, p. 23 (left); Tommy Gilliga / Newscom, p. 23; Cal Sport Media/ Alamy, p. 23 (right); Nick Wass/ AP Images, p. 23 (right); Larry French/ Getty Images, p. 26; Russell Tracy/ Southcreek Global/ ZUMA Press/ Alamy, pp. 28, 29 (mascot); Southcreek Global/ ZUMA Press/ Alamy, p. 29 (stadium).